Mount R
Fascinat

Peter Nielsen

This book is just one of a series of “Fascinating Facts For Kids” books. For more fascinating facts about people, history, animals and much more please visit:

www.fascinatingfactsforkids.com

Contents

The Idea

1. In 1889, South Dakota became the 40th state of America. It was a wonderful part of the country, full of dramatic scenery and natural beauty - but it was a long way from the major cities of America.

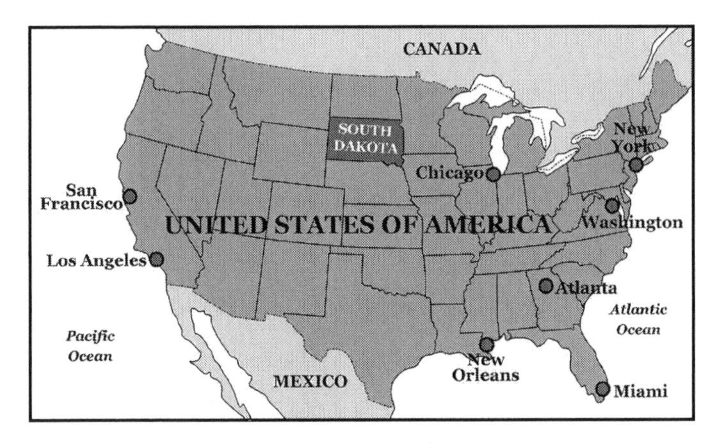

2. In the early 1920s, the state historian of South Dakota, Doane Robinson, wanted people from all over America to visit the state, and he came up with a bold plan to attract people there.

3. Robinson had heard about an ambitious project being undertaken at Stone Mountain in the southern state of Georgia. A massive monument was being carved into the mountain, and Robinson had plans for something similar in South Dakota.

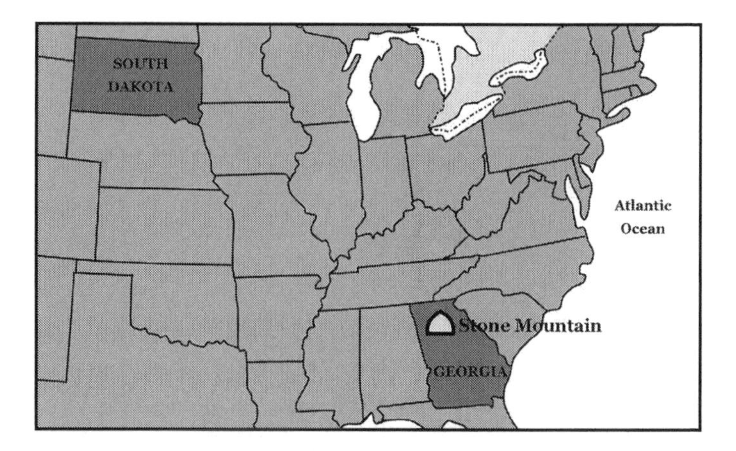

4. Robinson imagined a huge sculpture carved into South Dakota's Black Hills. He wanted carvings of Old West legends such as Buffalo Bill Cody and the Sioux Chief, Red Cloud.

Buffalo Bill Cody ***Red Cloud***

5. Robinson talked to other people about his plan, including US Senator Peter Norbeck. Norbeck was keen on the idea and got other government officials involved. There was soon enough interest for the project to begin.

Senator Peter Norbeck

6. Robinson needed someone to be in charge of the project, and he wrote to the sculptor at Stone Mountain inviting him to South Dakota to discuss his plans. The sculptor's name was Gutzon Borglum.

Gutzon Borglum

Gutzon Borglum

7. Gutzon Borglum was born in 1867, the son of Danish immigrants who had settled in Idaho in 1864.

8. As a child, Gutzon displayed great artistic ability, and decided that he would become an artist. When he was sixteen years of age he moved to San Francisco, California, to study painting.

9. At the age of twenty-three, Gutzon moved to France where he studied in Paris for three years. He was hugely influenced by one of his teachers, the great French sculptor Auguste Rodin, and decided to become a sculptor himself.

Auguste Rodin

10. In 1901, Gutzon moved back to America and started his career as a sculptor in New York City. He quickly established himself, and was commissioned to create many pieces of public art.

11. One of Gutzon Borglum's commissions was a huge statue of the head of Abraham Lincoln, which he carved from a six-ton block of marble. The statue was placed in the Capitol Rotunda in Washington D.C.

12. Borglum's statue of Lincoln led to a commission to create a monument of Civil War heroes carved into Stone Mountain in Georgia. It was here in August 1924 that Borglum received the letter inviting him to South Dakota.

13. Borglum had not been happy working on Stone Mountain, often arguing with the people he worked for. In 1925, he became so angry that he destroyed all the models he had created for the project, and left Georgia to head for South Dakota.

Mount Rushmore

14. When Borglum arrived in South Dakota, Doane Robinson took him into the Black Hills to see the place chosen for the statues to be carved - an area called "The Needles."

The Needles

15. The Needles was a group of giant granite pillars, but when Borglum saw them he decided it was not a suitable location. He believed the granite was not strong enough and that the tall, thin rocks were the wrong shape for large human figures. A new site would have to be found.

16. In September 1925, Borglum visited South Dakota for the second time. He climbed the highest mountain in the Black Hills, Harney Peak, and saw the perfect place for his sculpture - Mount Rushmore.

17. Mount Rushmore was 5,700 feet (1,740 m) high with a large area of strong, smooth granite. It also faced the Sun for most of the day, which made it the ideal place for Borglum's sculpture.

Mount Rushmore in 1905

The Four Presidents

18. Borglum didn't agree with Doane Robinson's idea of a monument glorifying the Old West. He decided that national heroes such as great United States presidents from the past would be more impressive.

19. Borglum chose four presidents that he admired and that he thought had been important in the history of the United States. They were George Washington, Thomas Jefferson, Abraham Lincoln, and Theodore Roosevelt.

20. George Washington was an obvious choice. He was a former soldier who became one of the Founding Fathers of the United States. He became the country's first president in 1789, holding the office until 1797.

George Washington

21. Thomas Jefferson, like Washington, was also a Founding Father of the United States. He wrote the original version of the Declaration of Independence, and was the country's third president from 1801 until 1809.

Thomas Jefferson

22. Abraham Lincoln is considered by many to be the best president the United States has ever had. He led the country through its most difficult time, the Civil War, and fought to abolish slavery.

Abraham Lincoln

23. Theodore Roosevelt was a controversial choice. He had died just a few years earlier in 1919, and many people thought he had been president too recently to be honored in Borglum's monument. But Borglum was a great admirer of Roosevelt and he got his way.

Theodore Roosevelt

Work Begins

24. Before work began on the mountain, Borglum made a plaster model of the four presidents. This model would be used as a guide when the sculpting of Mount Rushmore began.

Borglum's model

25. Every inch (2.5 cm) on the model would be the equivalent of twelve inches (30 cm) on the mountain. Borglum would use special equipment to transfer the measurements of the model onto the mountain to create carvings which were sixty feet (18 m) high.

26. Borglum studied the mountain carefully to make sure the rock was strong enough to be carved. When he found rock that was too soft or cracked, the model had to be altered to avoid these problem areas. Borglum had to change his model nine times as work went along.

27. Before the carving of Mount Rushmore could begin a lot of rock had to be removed. Borglum used dynamite to blast away 450,000 tons of rock which still lies at the foot of the mountain today.

28. After using the dynamite, Borglum sent a team of drillers and stone carvers onto the mountain who would chip away at the rock to create the monument.

29. An important part of the process was to make the rock surface smooth. Borglum used a team of men with special air-powered drills to get the rock as smooth as possible.

30. Borglum spent a lot of time at the mountain, studying it from all sides and in all types of weather. He made thousands of changes during the project. Even a tiny change could take days to complete.

31. The biggest change was to the carving of Thomas Jefferson's head. After eighteen months of drilling and carving, it was discovered that the rock was not strong enough to carry on. The whole head had to be blasted off with dynamite, and work restarted on another part of the mountain!

Working Conditions

32. Borglum hired hundreds of local men to work on the mountain. It was a hard and dangerous job, and some men were so afraid of working at such a great height that they quit after just one day!

33. Workers had to climb 760 steps at the start of every day to get to the top of the mountain. The drillers were then winched down the side of the mountain in harnesses to get to work on the drilling and carving.

Working on Washington's head

34. The granite was so hard that the drill bits needed replacing after every three feet (1 m) of drilling. A blacksmith at the bottom of the mountain sharpened around 400 replacement drill bits every day.

35. Despite the dangerous conditions and often freezing temperatures, there were no serious accidents during the construction. Borglum cared for the safety of his men and even told them to stop work every day at 10.00 a.m. for hot coffee and doughnuts. The coffee break was invented on Mount Rushmore!

Completion

The completed Mount Rushmore

36. Gutzon Borglum worked hard on the mountain for twelve years, from 1925-1937, but in 1938 his health began to fail and his son, Lincoln, took over as the new man in charge.

37. Like his father, Lincoln Borglum had worked on the project from the beginning, when he was a teenager. Since then he had worked on every part of the mountain and was the perfect person to take over.

38. Lincoln Borglum oversaw the carving of the head of Theodore Roosevelt - the last figure to be completed. The carving and drilling finally stopped in July 1939.

39. The two years from 1939-1941 were spent polishing the granite and applying the finishing touches, and on October 31, 1941, the Mount Rushmore sculpture was finally completed.

40. Gutzon Borglum died in Chicago on March 6, 1941, at the age of seventy-four and did not live to see his monument completed.

The Hall of Records

41. Gutzon Borglum wanted more than just statues carved into Mount Rushmore. He wanted to build a special room inside the mountain that would hold important historical documents and an explanation of why the monument was created.

42. Work began on the "Hall of Records" in July 1938 when a seventy-feet-long (21-m) tunnel was blasted into Mount Rushmore.

43. Unfortunately, the United States government, which was funding the project, had to order Borglum to stop work on the Hall of Records because the money was running out.

44. The unfinished hall sat empty and unused for sixty years until, in 1998, the Mount Rushmore National Memorial Society raised enough money to finish its construction.

45. Very few people are allowed into the "secret chamber." It is hoped that it will be discovered thousands of years from now, and that people from the future will learn about the history of the United States and why the Mount Rushmore monument was constructed.

Mount Rushmore Today

46. Mount Rushmore has become a national icon and is visited by around three million people every year. It has become one of America's most popular tourist attractions.

47. At the foot of Mount Rushmore is "The Avenue of Flags," where fifty-six flags are flown. The flags of every one of the fifty states of the United States are represented, along with the flags of Puerto Rico, the District of Colombia, and other US Territories.

View of Mount Rushmore from The Avenue of Flags

48. There is a lot you can do if you visit Mount Rushmore. There are Information Centers where you can learn all about the monument and the mountain. Tools used to create the monument are on display, as is the scale model made by Gutzon Borgnum.

49. Nowadays, Mount Rushmore is looked after by the National Park Service. Trained mountain climbers regularly inspect the carving for cracks, clean the stonework, and make sure the whole mountain is in good shape.

50. In Denmark, the people are very proud of Gutzon Borglum's Danish heritage. At Legoland in Billund, Denmark (the home of Lego), a model of Mount Rushmore is on display which is made from 1.5 million Lego pieces!

The Legoland model at Billund

Assorted Mount Rushmore Facts

51. The granite that the memorial is carved into erodes at the rate of one inch (2.5 cm) every 10,000 years, so barring a disaster such as an asteroid impact or another ice age, the carvings should be there for millions of years!

52. Each of the heads on the sculpture is the height of a six-story building. Each eye is eleven feet (3.3 m) wide, each mouth eighteen feet (5.5 m) across, and each nose is twenty feet (6 m) long. The workers said that if it rained, then nine people could shelter under George Washington's nose!

Washington's head

53. The mountain is named after a New York lawyer, Charles E. Rushmore. On an expedition in the area in 1885, Rushmore asked the locals the name of the mountain. They said it didn't have a name but they liked Rushmore so much that they decided to name it after him!

54. It took fourteen years to complete the Mount Rushmore monument, although because of times when there was no money or when the weather was too bad, only about six and a half of those years were spent actually working on the mountain.

55. The total cost of the project was $989,992 - the equivalent of around $16 million today. Most of the money came from the United States government.

56. Unlike the statues of Ancient Greece and Ancient Rome, whose eyes are flat and blank, the Mount Rushmore statues have eyes which look realistic. Borglum devised a technique of carving out a specially-shaped piece of rock in the middle of each eyeball, which catches the sunlight to make the eyes look almost real!

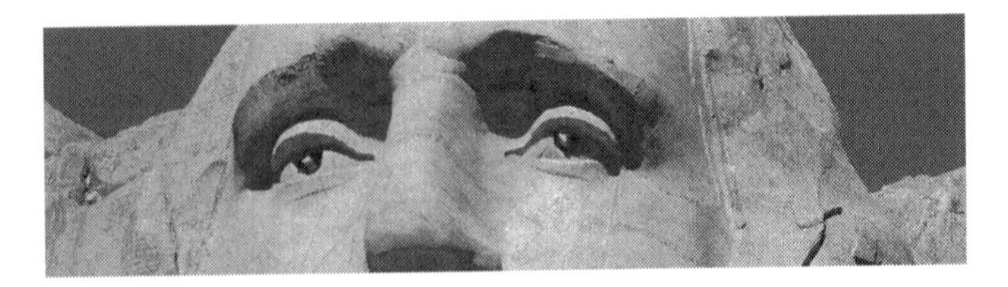

57. Not everyone was keen on the Mount Rushmore project. Some people in South Dakota thought that the natural beauty of the Black Hills would be ruined. The Lakota Sioux American Indians regarded the Black Hills as their land which had been stolen from them by the American government.

For more in the "Fascinating Facts For Kids" series, please visit:

www.fascinatingfactsforkids.com

Illustration Attributions

Buffalo Bill Cody
{{PD-1923}}
By Sarony - Sarony, 680 Broadway, New York, Public Domain, https://commons.wikimedia.org/w/index.php?curid=9534518

Red Cloud
Charles Milton Bell [Public domain]

Senator Peter Norbeck
By Unknown - http://bioguide.congress.gov/scripts/biodisplay.pl?index=N000132, Public Domain,https://commons.wikimedia.org/w/index.php?curid=1678439

Gutzon Borglum
Archives of American Art [Public domain]

Auguste Rodin
{{PD-1923}}
Public Domain, https://commons.wikimedia.org/w/index.php?curid=788446

The Needles
Doug Knuth [CC BY-SA 2.0 (https://creativecommons.org/licenses/by-sa/2.0)]

Mount Rushmore in 1905
{{PD-1923}}
By National Park Service - Taken from here where it is specifically credited as a NPS (National Park Service) photo., Public Domain, https://commons.wikimedia.org/w/index.php?curid=10646640

George Washington
{{PD-1923}}
By Gilbert Stuart - http://www.clarkart.edu/Collection/7577, Public Domain, https://commons.wikimedia.org/w/index.php?curid=591229

Thomas Jefferson
{{PD-1923}}
GoodFreePhotos
https://www.goodfreephotos.com

Abraham Lincoln
{{PD-1923}}
By Alexander Gardner - [1], Public Domain, https://commons.wikimedia.org/w/index.php?curid=42812335

Theodore Roosevelt
{{PD-1923}}
Pach Bros 1904

Borglum's model
{{PD-1923}}
By Rise Studio, Public Domain,
https://commons.wikimedia.org/w/index.php?curid=2917712

Working on Washington's head
{{PD-1923}}
Rise Studio, Rapid City, S. Dak. Copyright not renewed

View of Mount Rushmore from The Avenue of Flags
Chrishauck24 [CC BY-SA 3.0 (https://creativecommons.org/licenses/by-sa/3.0)] (changes made)

The Legoland model at Billund
Legoland Billund Resort [CC BY 3.0 (https://creativecommons.org/licenses/by/3.0)]

Washington's head
MichaelKirsh [CC BY-SA 4.0 (https://creativecommons.org/licenses/by-sa/4.0)]

Final image
Shelly Mead-Gaught [CC BY-SA 4.0 (https://creativecommons.org/licenses/by-sa/4.0)]

Made in the USA
Monee, IL
30 August 2021